Creating Yeast Doughs & Quick Breads

Megan Borgert-Spaniol

Abdo & Daughters
MIDDLE GRADE NONFICTION
An imprint of Abdo Publishing
abdobooks.com

ABDOBOOKS.COM

Published by Abdo Publishing, a division of ABDO, PO Box 398166, Minneapolis, Minnesota 55439. Copyright © 2024 by Abdo Consulting Group, Inc. International copyrights reserved in all countries. No part of this book may be reproduced in any form without written permission from the publisher. Abdo & Daughters™ is a trademark and logo of Abdo Publishing.

Printed in the United States of America, North Mankato, Minnesota
052023
092023

Design: Aruna Rangarajan and Emily O'Malley, Mighty Media, Inc.
Production: Mighty Media, Inc.
Editors: Jessica Rusick and Ruthie Van Oosbree
Recipes: Megan Borgert-Spaniol
Cover Photographs: Mighty Media, Inc.; Shutterstock Images
Interior Photographs: Claire H/Wikimedia Commons, p. 6 (top left); iStockphoto, pp. 4, 5 (top), 15 (skillet), 18 (middle left, bottom left, bottom right), 19 (all), 20 (all), 21 (top left, top right), 22, 26, 28, 29 (bottom), 54 (bottom right), 55 (all), 56, 57, 58, 59, 60, 61 (bottom); Mighty Media, Inc., pp. 23 (kneading steps), 24, 25, 30 (bread), 32 (all), 33 (all), 34–35, 36 (cornbread piece & pan), 38, 39, 40–41, 42 (focaccia), 44, 45, 46–47, 48 (loaf), 50, 51, 52, 53; Shutterstock Images, pp. 3, 5 (bottom), 6 (top right, bottom), 7, 8 (all), 9, 10, 11 (all), 12 (all), 13 (all), 14, 15, 16 (all), 17 (all), 18 (onions, top), 21 (bottom), 23 (top, middle right, bottom right), 24 (top), 25 (middle right, bottom right), 27 (all), 29 (top), 30 (background), 36 (background), 42 (background), 48 (background), 54, 58 (top), 61
Design Elements: Shutterstock Images

The following manufacturers/names appearing in this book are trademarks: KitchenAid® and Rostfrei™

Library of Congress Control Number: 2022948832

PUBLISHER'S CATALOGING-IN-PUBLICATION DATA

Names: Borgert-Spaniol, Megan, author.
Title: Bread workshop: creating yeast doughs & quick breads / by Megan Borgert-Spaniol
Other title: creating yeast doughs & quick breads
Description: Minneapolis, Minnesota : Abdo Publishing, 2024 | Series: Kitchen to career | Includes online resources and index.
Identifiers: ISBN 9781098291372 (lib. bdg.) | ISBN 9781098277833 (ebook)
Subjects: LCSH: Food--Juvenile literature. | Cooking--Juvenile literature. | Bread--Juvenile literature. | Baking--Juvenile literature. | Baked products--Juvenile literature. | Bread industry--Juvenile literature. | Dough--Juvenile literature. | Occupations--Juvenile literature.
Classification: DDC 641.815--dc23

CONTENTS

Making a Career in the Kitchen 5

The Basics 7

Getting Started 11

◆ **Banana Bread** 31
◆ **Corn Bread** 37
◆ **Rosemary Focaccia** 43
◆ **Brioche Loaf** 49

Presentation & Beyond 54

Careers in the Kitchen 57

Glossary 62

Online Resources 63

Index 64

MAKING A CAREER IN THE KITCHEN

Are you fascinated by the way flour and water combine to form dough? Do you love experimenting with recipes and making tweaks to improve them? Can you see yourself waking up early, putting on an apron, and baking dozens of loaves of bread for others to enjoy? If your answer to these questions is yes, you might be suited to a career as a bread baker.

Becoming a baker takes a lot of training and hard work. It takes dedication to craft, quality, and safety. But if you have a passion for baking bread, you may find that the dedication comes naturally and the hard work is worthwhile.

In this book, you'll learn about the history of bread and how bread making has changed over time. You'll become familiar with basic ingredients, tools, and techniques used to bake bread. You'll practice using these ingredients, tools, and techniques in a few basic recipes. Then, you'll try your hand at following your own tastes and inspirations to modify recipes. Finally, you'll learn how you might turn your passion for baking bread into a career.

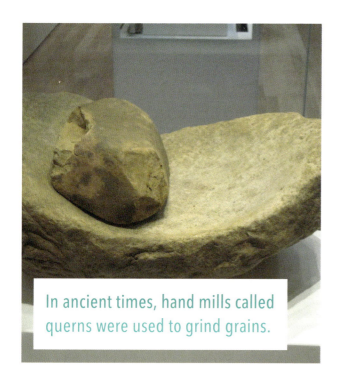

In ancient times, hand mills called querns were used to grind grains.

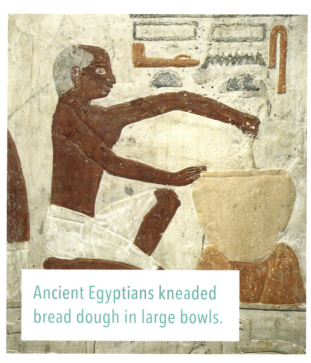

Ancient Egyptians kneaded bread dough in large bowls.

Sourdough starter is a common leavening agent made by mixing flour and water. Yeast and bacteria break down the mixture, adding air and flavor.

THE BASICS

INTRODUCTION TO BREAD

Bread is a baked food product that, in its simplest form, is made of grain and water. It is a staple food around the world that comes in the form of flatbreads, loaves, rolls, buns, and more. Bread can be sweet or savory or both. Wheat is the most popular grain used to make bread. But bread is also made using corn, barley, rye, millet, buckwheat, and other grains.

Humans have been baking bread for tens of thousands of years. About 10,000 years ago, bakers in Egypt used stones to crush wheat and barley to make flatbreads. In later centuries, water mills and windmills were used to grind grains. During the Industrial Revolution, automated mills were invented. Later on, steam-powered mills ground grains using steel rollers rather than stones.

As grain milling advanced over the years, bread leavening also evolved. Historians believe ancient Egyptians made leavened bread by letting the dough sit out before baking it. Wild yeast cells in the air landed on the dough and fed on sugars in it. As the yeast cells fed, they produced carbon dioxide, creating gas bubbles in the dough. This led to soft, risen bread. Bakers began to set aside a small portion of each batch of dough. This portion was used to leaven, or raise, the next batch of dough.

In colonial America, some bakers leavened their breads with brewer's yeast. This yeast was a by-product of the beer-brewing process. In the 1800s, Austrian chemists found a way to mass-produce yeast. Austrian Charles Fleischmann immigrated to the United States and began selling compressed yeast. In the 1940s, Fleischmann's company introduced active dry yeast. Dried yeast granules could be activated with warm water. The product made it possible for more people to enjoy baking fresh bread.

Brewer's yeast has a bitter flavor. It is used in savory breads.

Wonder Bread debuted in 1921. It is made with processed flour.

By the second half of the 1900s, bread was being mass-produced in the United States. Wheat flour was highly processed with chemicals and additives, making bread whiter, softer, and more shelf stable. As low-carbohydrate diets grew popular in the early 2000s, many people avoided bread, especially white bread that was high in carbohydrates and low in nutritional value.

Meanwhile, the 2010s brought a new appreciation for handmade breads formed with basic ingredients and using traditional methods. Whole grain loaves were popular for their nutritional value, while sourdough loaves were esteemed for their slow fermentation process.

In 2020, toward the start of the COVID-19 pandemic, many people challenged themselves to make sourdoughs and other breads while they were stuck at home.

Modern bread bakers experiment with countless combinations of grains, flavors, and fermentation methods. In the following pages, you'll learn about common ingredients, tools, and techniques used in bread making. Then you'll be ready to get baking!

As bread bakes, heat and steam cause starches on its surface to burst. The starches harden into a crispy and crackly crust.

GETTING STARTED

INGREDIENTS

Get familiar with some of the ingredients you'll see in this book's recipes.

BAKING POWDER & BAKING SODA

Baking powder and baking soda are leaveners used in quick breads. When mixed with liquid, they create carbon dioxide gas.

BUTTER & OIL

Butter and oil are fats. They give breads a rich taste and soft texture. For baking, use unsalted butter unless a recipe calls specifically for salted butter. Breads that use oil often call for neutral oils, such as vegetable, canola, or grapeseed oil. But some breads, including focaccia, use olive oil for its fruity, herby flavor.

CORNMEAL

Corn that has been dried and ground is called cornmeal. It is coarser than flour. Cornmeal is a key ingredient in corn bread, a popular quick bread. It also adds a subtle texture and flavor to yeasted breads.

EGGS

Eggs help bind ingredients in doughs and batters. They also act as leaveners because their proteins trap air bubbles. The fats in eggs help make breads rich and soft.

FLOUR

The recipes in this book call for all-purpose flour. This is a blend of wheat flours used to bake a variety of products, from crusty breads to fluffy cakes. However, many bread recipes call for bread flour, which has a higher protein content than all-purpose flour. The extra protein results in a stronger structure and chewier texture.

MILK

Milk contains fat that helps make breads soft. If a recipe calls for milk, try to use whole or 2 percent. Some recipes call for buttermilk, which is slightly thicker and more acidic than regular dairy milk. Bakers use buttermilk for its tang, which balances out sweet flavors. You can make a substitute for buttermilk by combining 1 cup of milk and 1 tablespoon of white vinegar or lemon juice. Let the mixture sit for five minutes before use.

SALT

Salt is a mineral that adds its own flavor and enhances other flavors. If a recipe does not call for a specific type of salt, regular table salt will do. Some recipes call for kosher salt, which is made up of coarser grains than table salt. The focaccia recipe in this book calls for kosher salt as well as flaky sea salt. Flaky salt is usually sprinkled on top of foods to add small bursts of flavor and crunch.

SUGAR

Recipes that call for sugar are usually referring to granulated sugar, or white sugar. Some recipes call for brown sugar. It contains molasses, giving it a higher moisture content and more complex flavor than white sugar.

VANILLA EXTRACT

Pure vanilla extract is made by soaking vanilla beans in an alcohol solution. This pulls out the flavors of the vanilla beans and concentrates them in liquid form. Vanilla extract adds a subtle caramel flavor to sweetened breads.

YEAST

Yeast is a leavener used in bread doughs. The recipes in this book use active dry yeast. Bakers may also use instant yeast, brewer's yeast, and fresh yeast.

KITCHEN TOOLS

Get familiar with some of the supplies you'll see in this book's recipes.

CAST IRON SKILLET

A cast iron skillet gives corn bread a deliciously crisp and golden crust. If you don't have a skillet, a regular baking pan will do!

DOUGH SCRAPER

A dough scraper is a rectangular piece of steel with a handle. Its dull blade end is used for dividing yeast doughs. Some dough scrapers are made of plastic instead of metal. They are strong enough to cut through dough but also flexible enough to scrape dough out of bowls and off mixing equipment.

COOLING RACK

Cooling racks allow air to circulate around hot food, helping it cool faster than it would on a solid surface.

DOUGH HOOK ATTACHMENT

If you have a stand mixer, the dough hook is a curved attachment strong enough to handle thick bread dough. The hook works the dough in a way that mimics kneading. Many hand mixers also come with dough hook attachments.

ELECTRIC MIXER

Both stand mixers and handheld mixers use electricity to blend, whip, and knead for you. But it's possible to make breads without them. Use a wooden spoon or rubber spatula to stir quick bread batters. Knead yeast doughs by hand (see page 23 for kneading basics).

PASTRY BRUSH

A pastry brush is a soft-bristled brush used to spread egg wash over dough. If you don't have a pastry brush, you can do the same job with an unused paintbrush, the back of a spoon, or your fingers.

ROLLING PIN

Some yeast doughs, such as pizza dough and cinnamon roll dough, are flattened with a rolling pin. If you don't have a rolling pin, try using a reusable water bottle or thermos that has straight, smooth sides.

TOOTHPICKS

Toothpicks are helpful tools for testing doneness in quick breads. Simply insert a toothpick into the center of the quick bread and pull it back out. If the toothpick comes out clean or has a few dry crumbs on it, the bread is done. If the toothpick has wet batter on it, the bread needs more time in the oven.

TOWELS

Use clean, damp cotton towels to cover yeast doughs while they rise. Damp towels help trap moisture, keeping the dough from drying out.

WHISK

A whisk is used to thoroughly blend fine ingredients, such as flour, baking soda, and salt. A whisk is also good for incorporating air into ingredients, such as eggs or cream. For mixing doughs or thick batters, use a stronger tool, like a wooden spoon, rubber spatula, or electric mixer.

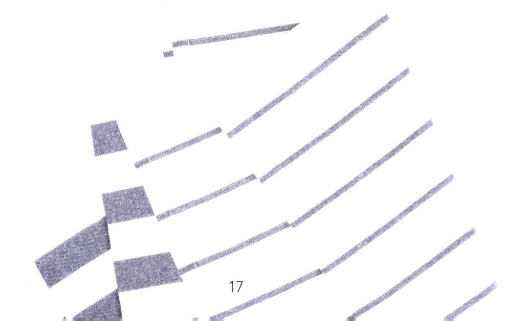

TERMS & TECHNIQUES

Get familiar with some of the terms and techniques you'll see in this book's recipes.

BATTER VERSUS DOUGH

A batter is a mix of wet and dry ingredients that is thin enough to be poured. Quick breads, such as banana bread and corn bread, start as batters that are stirred and poured into pans to bake.

A dough is a mix of wet and dry ingredients that is thick enough to hold its shape. Yeasted bread dough must be kneaded by hand or with an electric mixer.

CHOPPING VERSUS DICING

Chopping is a cutting technique that results in rough, uneven chunks of an ingredient.

Dicing is a more precise cutting technique that results in slightly smaller pieces of uniform size.

CREAMING BUTTER & SUGAR

Creaming is the process of working sugar into butter. It evenly distributes the sugar throughout the butter. It also incorporates air into the butter, increasing the butter's volume. This makes the final baked product light and fluffy. If you don't have an electric mixer, combine your butter and sugar with a fork, then use a wooden spoon to stir the mixture until it is soft and fluffy.

EGG WASH

An egg wash is a mix of egg and water or milk that is brushed over dough before baking. The wash gives the final product a nice golden color.

FLOURING THE WORK SURFACE

Most recipes call for doughs to be rolled out or kneaded on a floured surface. Start with a light, even sprinkle of flour over a clean, dry surface. If the dough starts to stick, sprinkle a little more flour onto the surface. Don't add too much! Otherwise, it will be harder to shape the dough.

GREASING THE PAN

Greasing a pan means covering it with a layer of fat before pouring batter or placing dough inside. The fat keeps the baked product from sticking to the pan. Unless a recipe calls for a specific fat, you can grease your pans with butter or any neutral oil, such as vegetable or canola oil. You can also use baking sprays, which contain oil mixed with flour.

LEAVENERS

Leaveners are rising agents. They create gases that expand inside dough or batter, causing it to rise as it bakes into bread.

MEASURING FLOUR

While professional bakers usually measure flour by weight, most recipes for home bakers include flour measurements by volume, or cups. To properly measure flour by volume, use a whisk to fluff the flour in the bag so it isn't tightly packed. Then spoon the flour into your measuring cup. Run the straight edge of a butter knife over the top of the cup to get rid of excess flour.

PREHEATING THE OVEN

Breads and most other baked goods rely on an initial blast of heat to kick-start their rise. That's why it's important to preheat your oven, or let it fully heat to the specified temperature, before you start baking.

PUNCHING DOWN THE DOUGH

When yeasted doughs rise, they fill with gas bubbles. Recipes often instruct you to "punch down the dough" after this rise. To do this, simply press gently into the dough with a fist to release all the built-up gas. After this, the dough is ready to be shaped.

RISING DOUGH

After a yeasted dough comes together, it is covered and set aside to rise. Yeast makes this rise possible because it releases carbon dioxide gas as it feeds on sugars in the dough. The amount of time it takes for a dough to rise depends on the type of bread. It also depends on the temperature. The warmer your kitchen, the faster your dough will rise.

SPONGE

A sponge is a portion of a bread dough's ingredients that are combined and allowed to rise before adding the remaining ingredients. Bakers use this method to achieve a complex flavor and light texture in their breads.

SOFTENING BUTTER

If a recipe calls for the butter to be softened, don't ignore it! Take your butter out of the refrigerator a couple hours before you start baking so the butter can come to room temperature. This makes it easier to cream the butter and sugar. If you need to soften butter in a hurry, cut it into smaller pieces and place it near a warm oven. Whatever you do, don't let the butter melt! This will affect the texture of your final product.

KNEADING BASICS

Part of the fun of making bread is the physical process of kneading the dough. If you don't have an electric mixer to help with the task or if you simply prefer to knead by hand, get familiar with some kneading basics.

Kneading techniques vary across recipes and bakers, but a basic push-and-fold movement is a good starting point for most doughs.

After punching down the risen dough, form it into a ball. Then place the dough ball on a clean surface. Only use flour if the dough is sticking to the surface.

Push the heel of your hand into the dough ball so it moves away from you along the surface.

Fold the far edge of the dough over itself and back toward you. Rotate the dough ball slightly before the next heel push.

Continue kneading until the dough is smooth and bounces back when you poke it. This can take 10 to 15 minutes.

KITCHEN PREP TIPS

- Have all your supplies out and ready before you begin. Gather all your ingredients on a tray or rimmed baking sheet. Then it's easy to slide everything out of the way if you need to make space.
- Wear an apron to protect your clothing. It will also serve as a hand towel.

KNEADING BRIOCHE

Brioche dough is especially sticky due to its high moisture and fat content. Because of this, it calls for a slightly modified kneading technique.

Use a rubber spatula to start combining the flour with the wet ingredients. When the dough has become too thick to stir, transfer it to a clean work surface. Use the basic push-and-fold technique (page 23) for about five minutes.

When the dough has become smooth and elastic, place it into a large bowl and add 2 tablespoons of softened butter. Use your fingers to poke dimples into the butter to help work it into the dough.

Fold an edge of the dough over itself and push it into the center. Then rotate the bowl and continue folding the dough over itself until the butter is fully incorporated.

Add another 2 tablespoons of butter. Repeat the dimpling and folding methods until you have added 8 tablespoons of butter. The process will be messy! Use a spatula to scrape the sides of the bowl when needed.

When all the butter is fully incorporated, transfer the dough to a lightly floured surface. Finish kneading with the basic push-and-fold technique for a few minutes. The dough should be smooth and elastic. Now it is ready to rise!

FOOD SAFETY TIPS

> Make sure your prep surface is clean and dry. Wash your hands with soap and water before and after you handle ingredients.
> Don't eat doughs containing uncooked flour or eggs.
> Place any leftover ingredients into containers with lids. Use tape and markers to label the container with the ingredient and the date. Then keep it somewhere you will easily see it so you don't forget about it.

CREATING IN THE KITCHEN

Recipes are great for learning how to bake bread. But as you get comfortable following recipes, you might start imagining ways to improve them.

Maybe there's a scone recipe that you think could be improved with buttermilk. Or maybe you'd like a little more salt in your go-to pizza crust recipe.

This book includes four formal bread recipes meant to help you practice working with different ingredients and techniques. Following each formal recipe is an informal companion. These companion recipes are less structured and provide fewer details. This leaves room for you, the baker, to follow your own tastes and preferences. If an informal recipe doesn't suit your taste, check out the accompanying "Experiment!" sidebar for additional ideas. With some thought and creativity, you can make any recipe your own way.

CONVERSION CHART

Standard	Metric
¼ teaspoon	1.25 mL
½ teaspoon	2.5 mL
1 teaspoon	5 mL
1 tablespoon	15 mL
¼ cup	60 mL
⅓ cup	80 mL
½ cup	125 mL
⅔ cup	160 mL
¾ cup	175 mL
1 cup	240 mL
325°F	160°C
350°F	180°C
375°F	190°C
400°F	200°C
425°F	220°C

RULES TO REMEMBER

As you start putting your own twist on recipes, keep these guiding principles in mind.

Master the basics first. Start out following recipes exactly as they are written. You'll better understand how ingredients combine and behave, and this knowledge will inform your decisions as you go off-book.

Every baker has their own methods. You might see another baker put their dough in a special basket to rise. Or, a baker may knead in a different way than you learned. This doesn't mean you have to use the same basket or knead the same way. If you can, ask a baker why their methods work for them. Test the methods yourself and decide what works best for you!

Experiments don't always go to plan. Don't be crushed if your bread didn't rise properly or burned a bit around the edges. If the results are still edible, don't let them go to waste! Instead, think of how you can make them tastier. If your corn bread is dry, brush it with honey butter. If your focaccia is crumbling, turn it into stuffing.

Baking is often called a precise science. But a recipe won't be ruined by an extra egg or a missed teaspoon of salt. Bakers are always tweaking and testing their recipes. Enjoy the process and take pride in the results.

> MAKE THIS!

BANANA BREAD

This popular quick bread gets its light sweetness and moisture from mashed bananas.

INGREDIENTS

- fat for greasing
- 2 cups all-purpose flour
- 1 teaspoon baking soda
- ½ teaspoon salt
- ½ cup (1 stick) unsalted butter
- ½ cup brown sugar
- 2 eggs
- ½ teaspoon vanilla extract
- 4 overripe bananas, mashed

SUPPLIES

- oven
- 8-by-4-inch (20.3-by-10.2 cm) loaf pan
- medium bowl
- whisk
- measuring cups and spoons
- large bowl
- electric mixer
- fork
- small bowl
- mixing spoon
- toothpick
- oven mitts
- cooling rack
- butter knife

1 Preheat the oven to 350°F and grease the loaf pan.

2 In a medium bowl, whisk together the flour, baking soda, and salt.

3

In a large bowl, cream the butter and brown sugar with an electric mixer until it is light and fluffy.

4

Mix the eggs and vanilla extract into the large bowl until the batter is smooth.

5

Use a fork to mash the bananas in a small bowl. Then stir them into the batter until just blended.

6

Add the flour mixture into the batter, stirring in a little bit at a time.

7

Pour the batter into the greased loaf pan and smooth it out evenly.

8

Bake the bread for 1 hour and 15 minutes. Test the bread's doneness by sticking a toothpick into the center of the loaf. The toothpick should come out clean or with a few dry crumbs on it. If needed, continue baking until a toothpick comes out clean.

9 Place the pan on a cooling rack for 20 minutes. Then run a butter knife along the edges of the bread to loosen it from the loaf pan.

10 Gently flip the pan over so the bread comes out onto the cooling rack. Turn the bread right side up and let it continue cooling.

MAKE IT YOUR WAY

CHOCOLATE NUT BANANA MUFFINS

Add a few extra ingredients to transform plain banana bread into delicious muffins!

When mixing the dry ingredients, replace up to ½ cup of the flour with cocoa powder.

EXPERIMENT!

Try making quick breads using other produce! Grated zucchini, applesauce, and pumpkin puree all bring flavor and moisture to quick breads. And they pair well with spices such as cinnamon and nutmeg.

When the batter is ready, stir in chocolate chips and chopped nuts.

Divide the batter into muffin cups and bake at 350°F. Check for doneness after about 20 minutes.

MAKE THIS!

CORN BREAD

Corn bread is a quick bread made with cornmeal and flour. Its crumbly texture makes it a delicious addition to any meal.

INGREDIENTS

- fat for greasing
- ¼ cup unsalted butter (½ stick)
- 1 cup all-purpose flour
- 1 cup yellow cornmeal
- ¼ cup brown sugar
- 1 tablespoon baking powder
- ½ teaspoon salt
- 1 cup buttermilk
- 1 egg
- ¼ cup honey

SUPPLIES

- oven
- 9-inch (22.9 cm) baking pan (circular or square)
- saucepan or microwave-safe bowl
- large bowl
- measuring cups and spoons
- whisk
- rubber spatula
- toothpick
- oven mitts
- cooling rack

1

Preheat the oven to 400°F and grease the pan.

2 Melt the butter in a saucepan over low heat or in the microwave for 15 seconds at a time. Set the melted butter aside to cool.

3

In a large bowl, whisk together the flour, cornmeal, brown sugar, baking powder, and salt.

4

Add the buttermilk, egg, and honey to the bowl and whisk to combine.

5

Use a rubber spatula to stir in the melted butter until just combined. Do not overmix.

6

Pour the batter into the greased pan and smooth it out evenly.

7

Bake the bread for 25 to 30 minutes or until it is golden on top. Test the bread's doneness by sticking a toothpick into the center of the loaf. The toothpick should come out clean. Let the bread cool on a cooling rack before serving.

[MAKE IT YOUR WAY]

SKILLET JALAPEÑO CHEDDAR CORN BREAD

Add some savory heat and sizzle to your pan of corn bread!

Place a cast iron skillet in the oven while the oven preheats. Slice and remove the seeds from a jalapeño. Then dice it. Use a cheese grater to make about 1 cup of shredded cheddar.

Stir the diced peppers and cheddar into the batter along with the melted butter.

Take the skillet out of the oven (careful, it's hot!). Grease the skillet before pouring in the batter. Bake at 400°F for 25 to 30 minutes.

EXPERIMENT!

Try stirring cooked corn into your batter for added texture. If you don't like jalapeño heat, try red bell peppers instead. For a completely different flavor combination, add cranberries and orange zest to your corn bread batter.

Make this!

ROSEMARY FOCACCIA

Focaccia is a flat Italian bread flavored with olive oil, salt, and herbs.

INGREDIENTS

- 1½ teaspoons active dry yeast
- 1 cup warm water
- 2 cups all-purpose flour
- 1 teaspoon kosher salt
- 4 tablespoons olive oil
- butter for greasing
- ½ tablespoon dried rosemary
- ½ tablespoon flaky sea salt

SUPPLIES

- whisk
- measuring cups and spoons
- large bowls
- rubber spatula
- bowl lid or plastic wrap
- refrigerator
- 9-inch (22.9 cm) baking pan (circular or square)
- oven
- oven mitts
- cooling rack

1

Whisk together the active dry yeast and warm water in a large bowl. Let the bowl sit for about five minutes.

2

Add the flour and kosher salt to the mixture. Use a rubber spatula to stir everything together until a shaggy dough forms.

3

Pour 2 tablespoons of olive oil into a second large bowl. Using a spatula, scrape the dough into the second bowl and turn the dough a few times so it is fully covered with the oil.

4 Cover the bowl with a lid or plastic wrap. Then put it in the refrigerator for about 12 hours to rise.

5 Grease the baking pan with butter. Pour in 1 tablespoon of olive oil.

6. Use the spatula to gently scrape the risen dough into a ball. Transfer the dough into the greased pan. Use greased hands to flip the dough ball over a few times so it is fully covered with the oil.

7. Let the dough rise, uncovered, until it has doubled in size. This may take a few hours. Test the dough by poking it. The dough is ready if it springs back slowly. If it springs back quickly, it needs more time to rest.

8. Preheat the oven to 425°F. Pour 1 tablespoon of olive oil over the top of the dough. Sprinkle the dried rosemary over the dough.

9. Use greased fingers to push deep dimples into the dough. As you do so, gently push the dough to the edges of the pan so it fills the entire bottom.

10. Sprinkle the flaky sea salt over the dough.

11. Bake the focaccia for 25 to 30 minutes. It should be golden brown.

12. Let the bread cool for ten minutes before removing it from the pan and placing it on a cooling rack.

[MAKE IT YOUR WAY]

GARDEN VEGGIE FOCACCIA

Customize your focaccia with your favorite vegetables and cheeses!

Chop up your favorite vegetables, such as tomatoes, bell peppers, olives, and red onion. Toss them in olive oil and balsamic vinegar.

EXPERIMENT!

Could you make focaccia the base of a pizza? Could you slice it up and grill the halves for sandwiches? Could you brush the warm focaccia with garlicky butter? Try out different preparations!

Before you dimple your focaccia dough, top it with the vegetables. If you'd like, add some feta or goat cheese. Then dimple the dough, pushing the toppings into it.

Sprinkle salt over the vegetables and dough before the pan goes into the oven.

MAKE THIS!

BRIOCHE LOAF

Brioche is a soft, rich French bread made with butter and eggs.

INGREDIENTS

- ½ cup whole milk
- 1½ teaspoons active dry yeast
- ¼ cup sugar
- 3 cups all-purpose flour, plus more for surface
- 4 eggs, room temperature
- 1 teaspoon salt
- ½ cup (1 stick) unsalted butter, softened
- fat for greasing
- 1 teaspoon water

SUPPLIES

- measuring cups and spoons
- microwave
- large bowl
- whisk
- damp towel
- small bowl
- mixer with dough hook attachment (optional)
- spatula and/or dough scraper
- 8-by-4-inch (20.3-by-10.2 cm) loaf pan
- oven
- pastry brush
- oven mitts
- cooling rack

1

Microwave the milk in a microwave-safe measuring cup 20 seconds at a time until it is warm but not hot. In a large bowl, whisk the milk with the yeast, sugar, and 1 cup flour. Cover the bowl with a damp towel and let the mixture sit for about 30 minutes. This is the sponge.

2 Whisk three eggs together in a small bowl. Add the eggs, 2 cups flour, and the salt to the sponge.

3

If you are kneading by hand, refer to pages 22 to 25. Otherwise, using the mixer with a dough hook attachment, beat the dough on low speed for about two minutes.

4

With the mixer on medium speed, add in the butter 1 tablespoon at a time. Let each tablespoon of butter fully incorporate into the dough before adding the next.

5

Scrape the dough off the hook and the sides of the bowl. Form it into a ball in the bowl. Cover the bowl with a damp towel. Let the dough rise for about an hour or until it has doubled in size. Scoop the dough onto a floured surface and punch down the dough. Divide it into three equal pieces. Roll each piece into a 15-inch (38.1 cm) rope.

6

8

6. Pinch the three long pieces together at the top. Braid the pieces, then pinch the bottoms together.

7. Grease the loaf pan. Place the braided loaf into the pan, tucking in the ends. Cover the pan with a damp towel and let the loaf rise until it has doubled in size. This should take about one hour.

8. Preheat the oven to 375°F. In a small bowl, whisk one egg with 1 teaspoon water. Brush the risen loaf with the egg wash.

9. Bake the loaf for 35 minutes or until it is a deep golden brown. Let the bread cool for ten minutes before removing it from the pan and placing it on a cooling rack.

MAKE IT YOUR WAY

BRIOCHE CINNAMON ROLLS

Turn brioche dough into yummy cinnamon rolls.

After you punch down the brioche dough, use a rolling pin to roll it out into a flat rectangle. Brush melted butter over the dough. Mix cinnamon and sugar (one part cinnamon to four parts sugar) and sprinkle the mix over the melted butter. Roll up the dough from one long end to the other.

EXPERIMENT!

Try other fillings for your brioche rolls, such as raspberry jam and white chocolate chips or cranberries and orange zest. Or, try turning your brioche dough into buns, donuts, and more!

Cut the roll of dough into pieces about 1 inch (2.5 cm) thick. Lay them in a greased 9-by-13-inch (22.9 by 33 cm) baking dish.

Cover the rolls and let them double in size. Then bake the rolls at 375°F for 20 minutes or until golden brown. Top the cooled rolls with a frosting of your choice!

PRESENTATION & BEYOND

Your bread is baked, but you're not done yet! It's time to think about how you want to display and serve your creation. Just as important is how you preserve any leftovers.

Serve banana bread as a partially sliced loaf to show off the bread's interior.

Consider serving cinnamon rolls with frosting on the side so everyone can frost to their liking. Or, place a dollop of frosting on each roll so some of the swirl is still visible.

Cut corn bread into square or triangular slices and serve with honey or butter.

Cut plain focaccia into thin slices. If you topped it with vegetables and cheese, leave it whole to show off your masterpiece!

Set out your brioche loaf unsliced on a cutting board. This showcases the braid and allows people to cut their own slice. Serve with jam.

STORING BREAD

If you plan to finish your leftover bread within a day or two, store it at room temperature in a sealed container. Avoid storing most breads in the refrigerator, where the cool temperature will dry out the bread. The freezer is cold enough to preserve a bread's freshness for more than two days. Wrap bread in plastic wrap before freezing. Let frozen bread thaw at room temperature, or place it directly into a toaster or 350°F oven to reheat it.

SPECIAL CONSIDERATIONS

> Rolls or other breads topped with cream cheese frosting shouldn't sit at room temperature for more than a few hours. Consider only frosting the rolls you know you'll eat right away. Then store leftover frosting in the refrigerator. Otherwise, store frosted rolls in the freezer.
> Focaccia topped with cheese or vegetables also requires special consideration. If you'll be eating the focaccia within a day, place it in a sealed bag and store it in the refrigerator. Otherwise, store it in the freezer.

CAREERS IN THE KITCHEN

BECOMING A BREAD BAKER

As you gain more knowledge and experience as a baker, you might decide to turn your hobby into a living. There are many ways to pursue a career in bread baking!

FORMAL SCHOOLING
Culinary and technical schools offer baking programs that last six months to a few years. These programs offer instruction in breads and other baked goods. They also prepare students for work in professional kitchens.

APPRENTICESHIP
Professional kitchens offer hands-on experience through apprenticeships and internships. These positions are often part-time and unpaid.

ON-THE-JOB TRAINING
Some establishments hire employees with no formal training. New bakers learn from experienced coworkers. Often, a new baker's wages increase as they gain more experience.

SELF-TEACHING
Many professional bakers learned what they know by reading cookbooks, watching others, and practicing in their own kitchens.

BREAD BAKERS AT WORK

As a baker, you can work in a variety of establishments. Read about a few of them below. Think about which suit you best and why.

RETAIL BAKERIES
Retail bakeries produce, package, and sell baked goods directly to customers.

RESTAURANTS
Some restaurants employ full- or part-time bakers to produce breads and other baked goods for the menu.

HOME OR RENTED BAKERY
Some bakers operate out of their home kitchens and sell goods to small shops or at farmers markets. Be sure to know your local laws before starting a business from your home. Alternately, many bakers rent commercial kitchen spaces.

WHOLESALE BAKERIES
Wholesale bakeries are high-volume operations that produce baked goods to be sold in bulk to restaurants, grocery stores, and other establishments.

GROCERY STORE BAKERIES
Many grocery stores hire bakers to produce fresh breads and other baked goods to be sold at the store.

Depending on where you work, baking professionally can be drastically different from home baking. As you think about baking for a living, consider some of the tools, rules, and schedules of a professional baker.

TOOLS

The tools of a professional baker are built to produce large quantities of breads and other baked goods. Industrial mixers can knead more than 90 pounds (40.8 kg) of dough at a time. Commercial ovens and cooling racks hold dozens of loaves at a time. Commercial kitchens also order bulk ingredients, such as 50-pound (22.6 kg) bags of flour. Bakers must be able to safely lift these heavy supplies.

RULES

Professional bakers must uphold cleanliness and food safety standards. These standards range from wearing a uniform and keeping hair pulled back to properly storing ingredients and thoroughly cleaning equipment after use. Bakers must also follow rules to protect themselves from kitchen hazards, such as hot pans and wet floors.

SCHEDULES

Many professional bakers start working at 4 a.m. so their bread is fresh and ready to sell by 8 a.m. Some bakers work all night long, starting around midnight and finishing around sunrise. Retail bakeries and restaurants are especially busy during weekends, so most bakers work at least one weekend day.

Do What You Love!

Being a baker requires early hours, hard physical work, and attention to rules and details. These requirements can be difficult for home bakers to adjust to. But many professional bakers find the rewards of their work outweigh the difficulties. These rewards include being creative, getting exercise, and learning new skills.

Maybe your goal is to manage a commercial kitchen. Maybe you have your sights set on owning a small baking business. Or perhaps you are happy to keep baking as a hobby but not as a career. As long as you do what you love, you'll love what you do.

GLOSSARY

additive—something that is added to something else in small amounts.

apprenticeship—an arrangement in which a person learns a trade or a craft from a skilled worker.

by-product—something produced in the making or breaking down of something else.

carbohydrate—a substance made by plants, which serves as a major class of foods for animals. Sugar and starch are examples of carbohydrates.

COVID-19—a serious illness that first appeared in late 2019.

culinary—having to do with the kitchen or cooking.

dimple—a shallow indentation. To dimple is to make shallow indentations in something.

edible—safe to eat.

enhance—to increase or make better.

establishment—a place or organization where people do business.

fermentation—the gradual chemical process in which substances, especially bacteria or yeast, change sugar into alcohol and produce carbon dioxide.

granule—a small, firm particle of a substance. A granulated substance is made of many small particles.

incorporate—to include or work into.

industrial—of or having to do with factories and making things in large quantities.

Industrial Revolution—a period in England from about 1750 to 1850. It marked the change from an agricultural to an industrial society.

internship—a program that allows a student or graduate to gain guided practical experience in a professional field.

molasses—the thick, brown syrup obtained as sugarcane is processed into sugar.

pandemic—the worldwide spread of a disease.

retail—related to the selling of goods directly to customers. Businesses that sell goods directly to customers are called retailers.

technique—a method or style in which something is done.

wholesale—relating to businesses that sell things in large amounts, often directly to other businesses.

ONLINE RESOURCES

To learn more about careers in bread baking, please visit **abdobooklinks.com** or scan this QR code. These links are routinely monitored and updated to provide the most current information available.

INDEX

American colonies, 7
Austria, 7

bakeries, 58–59
baking powder, 11, 37–38
baking soda, 11, 17, 31–32
batter, 11, 16–20, 32–35, 39, 41
bread
  color, 8, 15, 19, 39, 45, 51, 53
  flavor, 7, 11–13, 15, 21, 27, 29, 31, 34, 37, 40–41, 43, 49
  texture, 7–8, 11–12, 15, 18, 21, 29, 31, 33–34, 37, 41, 49, 55
brioche, 24, 49, 52–53, 55
buns, 7, 52
butter, 11, 18–21, 24–25, 29, 31–33, 37–39, 41, 43–44, 46, 49–50, 52, 54

careers, 5, 57–59, 61
cast iron skillets, 15, 40–41
chopping, 18, 35, 46
conversion, 27
cooling racks, 15, 31, 33, 37, 39, 43, 45, 49, 51, 59
cornmeal, 11, 37–38
COVID-19 pandemic, 8
creaming, 18, 21, 32

dicing, 18, 40
doneness, 17, 33–34, 39
dough, 5, 7, 11, 13, 15–21, 23–25, 29, 44–45, 47, 49–53, 59
dough hook attachment, 15, 49–50
dough scraper, 15, 44, 49–50

education, 29, 57, 61
egg wash, 16, 19, 51
eggs, 11, 16–17, 19, 25, 29, 31–32, 37–38, 49–51
Egypt, 7
electric mixers, 15–16, 18, 23, 31–32, 49–50, 59

fermentation, 8
flatbread, 7
Fleischmann, Charles, 7
flour, 5, 8, 11–12, 17, 19–20, 23–25, 31–33, 35, 37–38, 43–44, 49–50, 59
flouring the work surface, 19, 23, 25, 50
focaccia, 11–12, 29, 43–47, 55
food safety, 5, 25, 59
France, 49

grain, 7–8, 12
greasing the pan, 19, 31–33, 37–39, 41, 43–45, 49, 51, 53

history, 5, 7–8

Industrial Revolution, 7
Italy, 43

kneading, 15–16, 18–19, 23–25, 29, 50, 59

leavening, 7–8, 11, 13, 20
loaves, 5, 7–8, 31–33, 39, 49, 51, 54–55, 59

measuring, 12, 20, 24–25, 27, 31, 35, 37, 40, 43–45, 49–50
milk, 12, 19, 27, 37–38, 49–50
milling, 7

oil, 11, 19, 43–46

pans, 15, 18–19, 31–33, 37–40, 43–45, 47, 49, 51, 59
pastry brushes, 16, 19, 29, 46, 49, 51–52
pizza, 16, 27, 46
preheating, 20, 32, 38, 40, 45, 51
presentation, 54–55
preservation, 54–55
protection, 23, 59

punching down the dough, 20, 23, 50, 52
push-and-fold, 23–25

recipes
  banana bread, 31–33
  brioche cinnamon rolls, 52–53
  brioche loaf, 49–51
  chocolate nut banana muffins, 34–35
  corn bread, 37–39
  garden veggie focaccia, 46–47
  rosemary focaccia, 43–45
  skillet jalapeño cheddar corn bread, 40–41
rolling pins, 16, 52
rolls, 7, 52–55

salt, 11–12, 17, 27, 29, 31–32, 37–38, 43–45, 47, 49–50
selling, 7, 58–59
sourdough, 8
spatulas, 16–17, 24–25, 37, 39, 43–45, 49
sponge, 21, 50
sugar, 7, 13, 18, 21, 31–32, 37–38, 49–50, 52

temperature, 20–21, 27, 32, 38, 45, 49, 51, 55
toothpicks, 17, 31, 33, 37, 39
towels, 17, 23, 49–51

United States, 7–8

vanilla extract, 13, 31–32

water, 5, 7–8, 16, 19, 25, 43–44, 49, 51
whisks, 17, 20, 31–32, 37–38, 43–44, 49–51

yeast, 7–8, 11, 13, 15–18, 20–21, 43–44, 49–50